The Necessity

The Necessity of Social Control

István Mészáros

AAKAR

The Necessity of Social Control
István Mészáros

© Author

First Published in India, 2013

ISBN 978-93-5002-239-9

All rights reserved. No part of this book may be reproduced or transmitted, in any form or by any means, without prior permission of the Publisher.

Published by
AAKAR BOOKS
28 E Pocket IV, Mayur Vihar Phase I, Delhi 110 091
Phone : 011 2279 5505 Telefax : 011 2279 5641
info@aakarbooks.com; wwww.aakarbooks.com

Printed at
Mudrak, 30 A, Patparganj, Delhi 110 091

For Donatella

Contents

	The Necessity of Social Control	9
1.	The Counter-factual Conditionals of Apologetic Ideology	11
2.	Capitalism and Ecological Destruction	15
3.	The Crisis of Domination	20
4.	From "Repressive Tolerance" to the Liberal Advocacy of Repression	33
5.	War if the Normal Methods of Expansion Fail	38
6.	The Emergence of Chronic Unemployment	44
7.	The Intensification of the Rate of Exploitation	48
8.	Capital's "Correctives" and Socialist Control	52
	Appendix	
	Structural Crisis Needs Structural Change	58
	References	78

The Necessity of Social Control[*]

In the deeply moving final pages of one of his last works Isaac Deutscher wrote:

> The technological basis of modern society, its structure and its conflicts are international or even universal in character; they tend towards international or universal solutions. And there are the unprecedented dangers threatening our biological existence. These, above all, press for the unification of mankind, which cannot be achieved without an integrating principle of social organization. ... The present ideological deadlock and the social status quo hardly serve as the basis either for the solution of the problems of our epoch or even for mankind's survival. Of course, it would be the ultimate disaster if the nuclear super-Powers were to treat the social status quo as their plaything and if either of them tried to alter it by force of arms. In this sense the peaceful co-existence of East and West is a paramount historic necessity. But the social status quo cannot be perpetuated. Karl Marx speaking about stalemates in past class struggles notes that they usually ended "in the common ruin of the contending classes". A stalemate indefinitely prolonged and guaranteed by a perpetual balance of nuclear deterrents, is sure to lead the contending classes and nations to their common and ultimate ruin. Humanity needs unity for its sheer survival; where can it find it if not in socialism?[1]

Deutscher concluded his work by passionately stressing: "de nostra re agitur". it is all our own concern. Thus it seems to me right to address ourselves on this occasion to some of the vital problems which stood at the centre of his interest towards the end of his life.

All the more so because the "status quo" in question is a historically unique status quo: one which inevitably involves the *whole* of mankind. As we all know from history, no status quo has ever lasted indefinitely; not even the most partial and localized ones. The permanence of a *global* status quo, with the immense and necessarily expanding dynamic forces involved in it, is a contradiction in terms: an absurdity which should be visible even to the most myopic of game-theorists. In a world made up of a multiplicity of conflicting and mutually interacting social systems in contrast to the fantasy-world of escalating and de-escalating chess-boards the precarious global status quo is *bound* to be broken for certain. The question is not "whether or not", but "by what means'? Will it be broken by devastating military means or will there be adequate social outlets for the manifestation of the rising social pressures which are in evidence today even in the most remote corners of our global social environment? The answer will depend on our success or failure in creating the necessary strategies, movements and instruments capable of securing an effective transition towards a socialist society in which "humanity can find the unity it needs for its sheer survival".

1

The Counter-factual Conditionals of Apologetic Ideology

What we are experiencing today is not only a growing polarization inherent in the global structural crisis of present-day capitalism but, to multiply the dangers of explosion, also the break-down of a whole series of safety valves which played a vital part in the perpetuation of commodity society.

The change that undermined the power of consensus politics, of the narrow institutionalization and integration of social protest, of the easy exportation of internal violence through its transference to the plane of mystifying international collisions, etc., has been quite dramatic. For not so long ago the unhindered growth and multiplication of the power of capital, the irresistible extension of its rule over all aspects of human life, used to be confidently preached and widely believed. The unproblematic and undisturbed functioning of capitalist power structures was taken for granted and was declared to be a permanent feature of human life itself, and those who dared to doubt the wisdom of such declarations of faith were promptly dismissed by the self-perpetuating guardians of the bourgeois hegemony of culture as "hopeless ideologists", if not much worse.

But where are now the days when one of President

12 The Necessity of Social Control

Kennedy's principal theorists and advisers could speak about Marx and the social movements associated with his name in terms like these:

> He [Marx] applied his kit-bag to what he could perceive of one historical case: the case of the British take-off and drive to maturity; ... like the parochial intellectual of Western Europe he was, the prospects in Asia and Africa were mainly beyond his ken, dealt with almost wholly in the context of British policy rather than in terms of their own problems of *modernization*. ... Marx created *a monstrous guide to public policy*. [Communism] is a kind of disease which can befall a transitional society if it fails to organize effectively those elements within it which are prepared to get on with the job of modernization. [In opposition to the Marxist approach the task is to create] in association with the non-Communist politicians and peoples of the preconditions and early take-off areas [i.e. the territories of neocolonialism] a partnership which will *see them through* into sustained growth on a political social basis which keeps open the possibilities of progressive democratic development.[2]

These lines were written hardly a decade ago, but they read today like prehistoric reasoning, although – or perhaps because – the author is the professor of Economic History at the Massachusetts Institute of Technology.

In this short decade we were provided with tragically ample opportunity to see in practice, in Vietnam and in Cambodia, as well as in other countries, the real meaning of the programme of "partnership" intended "to see the politicians of the early take-off areas through" to the disastrous results of such partnership,[3] under the intellectual guidance of "Brain Trusts" which included quite a few Walt Rostows: men who had the cynical insolence to call *Marx's* work "a monstrous guide to public policy". Inflated by the "arrogance of military power", they "proved", by means of tautologies interspersed with retrospective "deductions", that the American stage of economic growth is immune to all crisis,[4] and they argued, with the help of counter-factual conditionals, that the break in the chain of imperialism was merely an unfortunate mishap which, strictly speaking, should not have happened at all. For:

> if the First World War had not occurred, or had occurred a decade later, Russia would almost certainly have made a successful transition to modernization and rendered itself invulnerable to Communism.[5]

We might be tempted to rejoice at the sight of such a level of intellectual power in our adversaries, were it not terrifying to contemplate the naked power they wield in virtue of their willing submission to the alienated institutions which demand "theories" of this kind so as to follow, undisturbed even by the possibility of an occasional doubt, their blind collision-course. The hollow constructions which meet this demand of rationalization are built on the pillars of totally false – and often self-contradictory – premises like, for instance:

1. socialism is a mysterious – yet easily avoidable – disease which will befall you, unless you follow the scientific prescription of American modernization;

2. facts to the contrary are merely the result of mysterious – yet easily avoidable – mishaps; such facts (e.g. the Russian Revolution of 1917) are devoid of an actual causal foundation and of a wider social-historical significance;

3. present-day manifestations of social unrest are merely the combined result of Soviet aspirations and of the absence of American partnership in the societies concerned; therefore, the task is to check-mate the former by generously supplying the latter.

"THEORIES" resting on such foundations can, of course, amount to no more than the crudest ideological justification of aggressive American expansionism and interventionism.

This is why these cynical ideologies of rationalization have to be misrepresented as "objective social and political science" and the position of those who *see through* the unctuous advocacy of "seeing the politicians of the early take-off areas through" – by means of the "Great American Partnership" of massive military interventions – must be denounced as "nineteenth century ideologists".

The moment of truth arrives, however, when the "mishaps" of social explosion occur, even more mysteriously than in the "early take-off areas", in the very land of "supreme modernization" and higher than "high mass-consumption". namely in America itself. Thus, not only is the model of undisturbed growth and modernization shattered but, ironically, even the slogan of "sustained growth on a political and social basis which keeps open the possibilities of progressive, democratic development" ideologically backfires at a time when outcries against the violation of basic liberties and against the systematic disenfranchizing of the masses is on the increase. That we are not talking about some remote, hypothetical future but about our own days, goes without saying. What needs stressing, however, is that the dramatic collapse of these pseudo-scientific rationalizations of naked power marks the end of an era: not that of "the end of ideology" but of the end of the almost complete *monopoly* of culture and politics by anti-Marxist ideology successfully self-advertised up until quite recently as the final supersession of all ideology.

2

Capitalism and Ecological Destruction

A Decade ago the Walt Rostows of this world were still confidently preaching the *universal* adoption of the American pattern of "high mass-consumption" within the space of one single century. They could not be bothered with making the elementary, but of course necessary, calculations which would have shown them that in the event of the universalization of that pattern – not to mention the economic, social and political absurdity of such an idea – the ecological resources of our planet would have been exhausted well before the end of that century several times over. After all, in those days top-politicians and their Brain-Trusts did not ride on the bandwagon of ecology but in the sterilized space-capsules of astronautical and military fancy. Nothing seemed in those days too big, too far, and too difficult to those who believed – or wanted us to believe – in the religion of technological omnipotence and of a Space Odyssey round the corner.

Many things have changed in this short decade. The arrogance of military power suffered some severe defeats not only in Vietnam but also in Cuba and in other parts of the "American hemisphere". International power-relations have undergone some significant changes, with the immense development of China and Japan in the first place, exposing to ridicule the nicely streamlined calculations of escalation-experts who now have to invent not only an entirely new type of multiple-player chess game but also the kind of creatures willing to play it, for want of real-life takers. "The affluent society" turned out to be the society of suffocating *effluence*, and the allegedly omnipotent technology failed to cope even with the invasion of rats in the depressing slums of black ghettos. Nor did the religion of Space Odyssey fare any better, notwithstanding the astronomical sums invested in it: recently even the learned Dr. Werner von Braun himself had to link-up the latest version of his irresistible "yearning for the stars" with the prosaic bandwagon of pollution (so far, it seems, without much success).

"The God that failed" in the image of technological omnipotence is now revarnished and shown around again under the umbrella of universal "ecological concern". Ten years ago ecology could be safely ignored or dismissed as totally irrelevant. Today it must be grotesquely misrepresented and one-sidedly exaggerated so that people – sufficiently impressed by the cataclysmic tone of ecological sermons – can be successfully diverted from their burning social and political problems. Africans, Asians, and Latin Americans (especially Latin Americans) should not multiply at pleasure – not even at God's pleasure, if they are Roman Catholics – for lack of restraint might result in "intolerable ecological strains". That is, in plain words, it might even endanger the prevailing social relation of forces, the rule of capital. Similarly, people should forget all about the astronomical expenditure on armaments and accept sizeable cuts in their standard of living, in order to meet the costs of "environmental rehabilitation": that is, in plain words, the costs of keeping the established system of expanding waste-production well-oiled. Not to mention the additional bonus of making people at large pay, under the pretext of "human survival", for the survival of a socioeconomic system which now has to cope with deficiencies arising from growing international competition and from an increasing shift in favour of the parasitic sectors within its own structure of production.

THAT capitalism deals this way – namely its own way – with ecology, should not surprise us in the least: it would be nothing short of a miracle if it did not. Yet the exploitation of this issue for the benefit of "the modern industrial state" – to use a nice phrase of Professor Galbraith's – does not mean that we can afford to ignore it. For the problem itself is real enough, whatever use is made of it today.

Indeed, it has been real for quite some time, though, of course, for reasons inherent in the necessity of capitalist growth, few have taken any notice of it. Marx however – and this should sound incredible only to those who have repeatedly buried him as an "irretrievably irrelevant ideologist of nineteenth century stamp" – had tackled the issue, within the dimensions of its true social-economic significance, more than one hundred and twenty-five years ago.

Criticizing the abstract and idealist rhetoric with which Feuerbach assessed the relationship between man and nature, Marx wrote:

> Feuerbach ... always takes refuge in external nature, and moreover in nature which has not yet been subdued by men. But every new invention, every new advance made by industry, detaches another piece from this domain, so that the ground which produces examples illustrating such Feuerbachian propositions is steadily shrinking. The "essence" of the fish is its "existence", water – to go no further than this one proposition. The "essence" of the freshwater fish is the water of a river. But the latter ceases to be the "essence" of the fish and is no longer a suitable medium of existence as soon as the

river is made to serve industry, as soon as it is polluted by dyes and other waste products and navigated by steamboats, or as soon as its water is diverted into canals where simple drainage can deprive the fish of its medium of existence.[6]

This is how Marx approached the matter in the early eighteen forties. Needless to say, he categorically rejected the suggestion that such developments are inevitably inherent in the "human predicament" and that, consequently, the problem is how to *accommodate* ourselves[7] to them in everyday life. He fully realized, already then, that a radical restructuring of the prevailing *mode* of human interchange and control is the necessary prerequisite to an effective control over the forces of nature which are brought into motion in a blind and ultimately self-destructive fashion precisely by the prevailing, alienated and reified mode of human interchange and control. Small wonder, then, that to present-day apologists of the established system of control his prophetic diagnosis is nothing but "parochial anachronism".

To say that "the costs of cleaning up our environment must be met in the end by the community" is both an obvious platitude and a characteristic evasion, although the politicians who sermonize about it seem to believe to have discovered the philosophers' stone. *Of course* it is always the community of producers who meet the cost of everything. But the fact that it always *must* meet the costs does not mean in the least that it always *can* do so. Indeed, given the prevailing mode of alienated social control, we can be sure that it *will not be able* to meet them.

Furthermore, to suggest that the already prohibitive costs should be met by "consciously putting aside a certain proportion of the resources derived from extra growth" – at a time of nil growth coupled with rising unemployment

Capitalism and Ecological Destruction

and rising inflation – is worse than Feuerbach's empty rhetoric. Not to mention the additional problems necessarily inherent in increased capitalistic growth.

And to add that "but this time growth will be controlled growth" is completely beside the point. For the issue is not *whether or not* we produce under *some* control, but under what *kind* of control; since our present state of affairs has been produced under the "iron-fisted control" of capital which is envisaged, by our politicians, to remain the fundamental regulating force of our life also in the future.

And, finally, to say that "science and technology *can* solvè all our problems in the long run" is much worse than believing in witchcraft; for it tendentiously ignores the devastating social embeddedness of present-day science and technology. In this respect, too, the issue is not *whether or not* we use science and technology for solving our problems – for obviously we must – but whether or not we *succeed* in radically *changing* their *direction* which is at present narrowly determined and circumscribed by the self-perpetuating needs of profit maximization.

These are the main reasons why we cannot help being rather sceptical about the present-day institutionalization of these concerns. Mountains are in labour and a mouse is born: the super-institutions of ecological oversight turn out to be rather more modest in their achievements than in their rhetoric of self-justification: namely Ministries for the Protection of Middle-Class Amenities.

3

The Crisis of Domination

In the meantime, on this plane as well as on several others, the problems accumulate and the contradictions become increasingly more explosive. The objective tendency inherent in the nature of capital – its growth into a global system coupled with its concentration and increasingly greater technological and science-intensive articulation – undermines and turns into an anachronism the social/structural subordination of labour to capital.[8] Indeed, we can witness already that the traditional forms of hierarchical/structural embeddedness of the functional division of labour tend to disintegrate under the impact of the ever-increasing concentration of capital and socialization of labour. Here I can merely point to a few indicators of this striking change:

1. The escalating vulnerability of contemporary industrial organization as compared to the nineteenth century factory. (The so-called "wild-cat strikes" are inconceivable without the underlying economic and technological processes which both induce and enable a "handful" of workers to bring to a halt even a whole branch of industry, with immense potential repercussions.)
2. The economic link-up of the various branches of

industry into a highly stretched system of closely interdependent parts, with an ever-increasing imperative for safeguarding the *continuity of production* in the system as a whole. (The more the system is stretched as regards its cycle of reproduction, the greater is the imperative of continuity, and every disturbance leads to more stretch as well as to an ever-darkening shadow of even a temporary break-down in continuity.) There are increasingly fewer "peripheral branches", since the repercussions of industrial complications are quickly transferred, in the form of a chain-reaction, from any part of the system to all its parts. Consequently, there can be no more "trouble-free industries". The age of paternalistic enterprise has been irretrievably superseded by the rule of "oligopolies" and "super-conglomerates".

3. The growing amount of socially "superfluous time" (or "disposable time"),[9] customarily called "leisure", makes it increasingly absurd, as well as practically impossible, to keep a large section of the population living in apathetic ignorance, divorced from their own intellectual powers. Under the impact of a number of weighty socioeconomic factors the old mystique of intellectual elitism has already disappeared for good. Also, side by side with a growing intellectual unemployment both potential and actual as well as a worsening of the cleavage between what one is supposed to be educated for and what one actually gets in employment opportunities, it becomes more and more difficult to maintain the traditionally unquestioning subordination of the vast majority of intellectuals to the authority of capital.

4. The worker as a consumer occupies a position of

increasing importance in maintaining the undisturbed run of capitalist production. Yet, he is as completely excluded from control over both production and distribution as ever as if nothing had happened in the sphere of economics during the last century or two. This is a contradiction which introduces further complications into the established productive system based on a socially stratified division of labour.

5. The effective establishment of capitalism as an economically interlocking world system greatly contributes to the erosion and disintegration of the traditional, historically formed and locally varying, partial structures of social and political stratification and control, without being able to produce a unified system of control on a world-wide scale. (So long as the power of capital prevails, "world-government" is bound to remain a futurologist pipe-dream.) The "crisis of hegemony, or crisis of the State in all spheres" (Gramsci) has become a truly international phenomenon.

In the last analysis all these points are about the question of *social control.*

In the course of human development, the function of social control had been alienated from the social body and transferred into capital which, thus, acquired the power of grouping people in a hierarchical structural/functional pattern, in accordance with the criterion of a greater or lesser share in the necessary control over production and distribution.

Ironically, though, the objective trend inherent in the development of capital in all spheres from the mechanical fragmentation of the labour process to the creation of automated systems, from local accumulation of capital to its concentration in the form of an ever-expanding and self-saturating world system, from a partial and local to a comprehensive international division of labour, from limited consumption to an artificially stimulated and manipulated mass-consumption, in the service of an ever-accelerating cycle of reproduction of commodity-society, and from "free time" confined to a privileged few to the mass production of social dynamite, in the form of "leisure", on a universal scale carries with it a result diametrically opposed to the interest of capital. For in this process of expansion and concentration, the power of control invested in capital is being *de facto* re-transferred to the social body as a whole, even if in a necessarily irrational way, thanks to the inherent irrationality of capital itself.

That the objectively slipping control is described from the standpoint of capital as "holding the nation to ransom", does not alter in the least the fact itself. For nineteenth century capitalism could not be "held to ransom" even by an army of so-called "troublemakers", let alone by a mere "handful" of them.

Here we are confronted with the emergence of a fundamental contradiction: that between an effective loss of control and the established form of control, capital, which, by its very nature, can be nothing but control, since it is constituted through an alienated objectification of the function of control as a reified body apart from and opposed to the social body itself. No wonder, therefore, that in the last few years the idea of workers' control has been gaining in importance in many parts of the world.

The social status quo of not so long ago is rapidly and dramatically disintegrating in front of our very eyes – if only we are willing to open them. The distance between Uncle Tom's Cabin and the beleaguered headquarters of black militancy is *astronomical*. And so are the distances from the depressing working class apathy of the post-war period to today's, even officially admitted, growing militancy on a world-wide scale; from graciously granted presidential "participation" to the Paris street fights; from a badly divided and narrowly wage-orientated Italian trade union movement to the unity necessary for the organization of a political general strike; or, for that matter, from the monolithic, unchallenged rule of Stalinism to the elemental eruption of massive popular dissent in Poland, in Hungary, in Czechoslovakia, and recently in Poland again. And yet, it did not take anything like light-years – not even light-minutes – to travel such astronomical distances.

Not so long ago the "scientific" ideology of gradualist "social engineering" – as opposed to the "religious holism" of revolutionary change and socialism – enjoyed an almost completely monopolistic position not only in educational and cultural institutions but also in the ante-chambers of political power. But, good heavens, what are we witnessing today? The dramatic announcement of the need for a "major revolution" by none other than President Nixon himself, in his recent State of the Union message; followed by the Shah of Persia's warning that he is going to spearhead the "rebellion of the have-nots against the haves".

And Mr. Wilson too, who mysteriously lost the word "socialism" from his vocabulary the very minute he walked through the front door of 10 Downing Street – and it just could not be found, though his entire team of experts and advisers as well as cabinet colleagues were looking for it for almost six years through the powerful spectacles of "pragmatic modernization", supplied completely free of prescription charges – mysteriously found the word again after leaving the Prime Ministerial residence by the back door. Indeed, in one of his public speeches he even cracked a joke about the "Pentagon hunting for communists under the sea-bed", though at the same time by a slight fit of amnesia forgetting that he was himself fishing for communists under the Seamen's bed not that long ago.

President Nixon: a new *revolutionary;* the Shah of Persia: *leader of the world rebellion of the have-nots;* and Mr. Wilson: an indomitable *crusader against the Pentagon's anti-communist crusades.* I wonder what might come next. (I did not have to wonder for long: only a few days after this lecture was delivered, Mr. Heath – yet another "pragmatic modernizer", of Rolls Royce fame – hastened to add, in the truest spirit of consensus-politics, his name to our illustrious list: as a vigorous *champion of nationalization.*)

However, even metamorphoses of this kind are indicative of powerful pressures whose nature simply cannot be grasped through the mystifying personalization of the issues as expressed in hollow concepts like "bridging the credibility gap", "acquiring a new image", etc. The hypothesis that politicians break their promises because they are "devious" and because they "lack integrity", only begs the question, at best. And the suggestion that they change their slogans and catchphrases, because "they need to change their image" is the emptiest of the whole range of tautologies produced by the post-war boom of behaviourist and functionalist "Political Science". Concepts of this kind are nothing more than pretentiously inflated rationalizations of the practice of self-advertising through which the advertising media sell their services to credulous politicians. As Mr. Wilson himself can testify: the simple and strictly quantifiable truth is that the psephologist "credibility gap" between this kind of "scientific" electoral victory forecast and the painfully final result of defeat exactly equals the distance between the front door and the back door of 10 Downing Street.

If the tone of traditional politics is changing today, it is because the objective contradictions of our present-day situation cannot be repressed any longer either by means of naked power and brute force or through the soft strangulation supplied by consensus politics. Yet, what we are confronted with is but an unprecedented crisis of social control on a world scale, and not its solution. It would be highly irresponsible to lull ourselves into a state of euphoria, contemplating a "socialist world-revolution round the corner".

The power of capital, in its various forms of manifestation, though far from being exhausted, does no longer reach far enough. Capital – since it operates on the basis of the myopic rationality of narrow self-interest, of *bellum omnium contra omnes:* the war of each against all, is a mode of control which – is apriori incapable of providing the comprehensive rationality of an adequate social control. And it is precisely the need for the latter which demonstrates its dramatic urgency with the passing of every day.

The awareness of the limits of capital has been absent from all forms of rationalization of its reified needs, not only from the more recent versions of capitalist ideology. Paradoxically, however, capital is now forced to take notice of some of these limits, although, of course, in a necessarily alienated form. For now at least the absolute limits of human existence – both at the military and at the ecological plane – *must* be sized up, no matter how distorting and mystifying are the measuring devices of a capitalist social-economic accountancy. Facing the dangers of a nuclear annihilation on one side and of an irreversible destruction of the human environment on the other, it becomes imperative to devise practical alternatives and remedies whose failure is rendered inevitable by the very limits of capital which have now collided with the limits of human existence itself. It goes without saying, the limits of capital carry with them an approach which tries to exploit even these vital human concerns in the service of profit-making. The lunatic – but, of course, capitalistically "rational" – theories (and associated practices) of "escalating" war-industry as the ultimate safeguard against war have dominated "strategic thinking" now for quite some time. And recently we could observe the mushrooming of parasitic enterprises – from the smallest to the largest in size – which all try to cash in on our growing awareness of the ecological dangers. (Not to mention the ideological-political operations associated with the same issues).[10]

All the same, such manipulations do not solve the issues at stake. They can only contribute to their further aggravation. Capitalism and the rationality of comprehensive social planning are radically incompatible. Today, however, we witness the emergence of a fundamental contradiction, with the gravest possible implications for the future of capitalism: for the first time in human history the unhampered dominance and expansion of the inherently irrational capitalist structures and mechanisms of social control are being seriously interfered with by pressures arising from the elementary imperatives of mere survival. And since the issues themselves are as unavoidable as the contradiction between the need for an adequate social control and the narrow limits of capitalist accountancy is sharp, the necessary failure of programmes of short-sighted manipulation – in a situation which demands far-reaching and consciously coordinated efforts on a massive scale – acts as a catalyst for the development of socialist alternatives.

And this is far from being the sum total of the rising complications. The mass production of disposable time mentioned earlier is now coupled not only with expanding knowledge, but also with growing consciousness of the contradictions inherent in the practically demonstrated failures, as well as with the development of new modes and means of communication potentially *capable* of bringing to light the massive evidence for the eruption of these contradictions.[11]

At the same time, some of the most fundamental institutions of society are affected by a crisis never even imagined before.

The power of religion in the West has almost completely evaporated a long time ago, but this fact has been masked by the persistence of its rituals and, above all, by the effective functioning of substitute-religions, from the abstract cult of "thrift" in the more remote past to the religion of "consumer-sovereignty", "technological omnipotence", and the like, in more recent decades.

The structural crisis of education has been in evidence now for a not negligible number of years. And it is getting deeper every day, although its intensification does not necessarily take the form of spectacular confrontations.

And the most important of them all: the virtual *disintegration* of present-day family – this cell of class society – presents a challenge to which there cannot conceivably be formal-institutional answers, whether in the form of "amending the law of trespass" or in some more ruthlessly repressive form. The crisis of this institution assumes many forms of manifestation, from the hippy cults to widespread drug-taking; from the "Women's Liberation Movement" to the establishment of utopian enclaves of communal living; and from the much advertised "generation-conflict" to the most disciplined and militant manifestations of that conflict in organized action. Those who have laughed at them in the past had better think again. For whatever might be their relative weight in the total picture today, they are potentially of the greatest significance without one single exception.

Equally significant is the way in which the stubborn persistence of wishful thinking misidentifies the various forms of crisis. Not only are the manifestations of conflict ignored up to the last minute; they are also misrepresented the minute after the last. When they cannot be swept any longer under the carpet, they are tackled merely as *effects* divorced from their *causes*. (We should remember the absurd hypotheses of "mysterious diseases" and of "events devoid of any foundation" mentioned above.)

Characteristically, we find in a recent book on economics, at the foot of a page which calls for "reducing industrial investments in favour of a large-scale replanning of our cities, and of restoring and enhancing the beauty of many of our villages, towns and resorts", the following story:

> The recent electric-power breakdown in New York, obviously to be deplored on grounds of efficiency, broke the spell of monotony for millions of New Yorkers. People enjoyed the shock of being thrown back on their innate resources and into sudden dependence upon one another. For a few hours people were freed from routine and brought together by the dark. Next-door strangers spoke, and gladdened to help each other. There was room for kindness. The fault was repaired. The genie of power was returned to each home. And as the darkness brought them stumbling into each other's arms, so *the hard light scattered them again*. Yet someone was quoted as saying, "This should happen at least once a month".[12]

The only thing one does not quite understand: why not "at least once a week"? Surely the immense savings on all that unused electricity would more than cover the costs of a "large-scale replanning of our cities, and of restoring and enhancing the beauty of many of our villages, towns and resorts". Not to mention the supreme benefits inherent in practising the new-found virtue of unlit-skyscraper-corridor-brotherhood regularly on a weekly basis. For apparently it is not the mode of their social relationships that "scatters people" apart, but the technological efficiency and monotony of "hard light". Thus, the obvious remedy is to give them less "hard light" and all the unwanted problems disappear for good. That the production of "hard light" is a social necessity, and cannot be replaced even for the duration of periodic rituals by soft candle-light, is a consideration evidently unworthy of the attention of our champions in romantic day-dreaming.

To put it in another way: this approach of wishful thinking is characterized by a curt dismissal of all those expectations which the system cannot meet. The representatives of this approach insist, with unfailing tautology, that such expectations are not the manifestation of social and economic contradictions but merely the *effects* of "rising expectations". Thus, not only is the challenge of facing up to the *causal foundations* of frustrated expectations systematically evaded but at the same time this evasion itself is very conveniently "justified", i.e. rationalized.

The fact is, however, that we are concerned here with an internal contradiction of a system of production and control: one which cannot help raising expectations even to the point of a complete breakdown in satisfying them. And it is precisely at such points of breakdown that Quixotic remedies and substitutes are advocated with so much "humanitarian" passion. Up until, or prior to, these points of crisis and breakdown, no one in his right mind is supposed to question the superior wisdom of "cost-effectiveness", "business-sense", "technological efficiency", "economic motives", and the like. But no sooner does the system fail to deliver the goods it so loudly advertised the moment before confidently indicating, prior to the eruption of structural disturbances, its own ability to cater for expanding expectations as the self-evident proof of its superiority over all possible alternative modes of production and social control its apologists immediately switch from preaching the religion of "cost-effectiveness" and "economic motives" to sermonizing about the need for "self-denial" and "idealism", untroubled not only by their sudden change of course but also by the rhetorical unreality of their wishful "solutions".

Thus, beyond the horizon of "artificial obsolescence" we are suddenly confronted with "theories" advocating the planning of artificial powercuts, the production of artificial scarcity both material and as an antidote to too much "disposable time" which involves the danger of an increasing social consciousness; of space-solidarity and artificially manipulated suspense, etc. Indeed, at a time of dangerously rising unemployment there are still with us antediluvian "theorists" who wish to counteract the complications arising from a total lack of aim in saturated commodity-existence by seriously advocating the production of artificial unemployment and hardship, topping it all up with nostalgic speeches about lost religions and about the need for a brand-new artificial religion. The only thing they fail to reveal is how they are going to devise also an artificial being who will systematically fail to notice the grotesque artificiality of all these artificialities.

Once upon a time it suited the development of capitalism to let out of the bottle the genie of a ruthless conversion of everything into marketable commodities, even though this deed necessarily carried with it the undermining and the ultimate disintegration of religious, political and educational institutions which were vital to the control mechanism of class society. Today, however, the status quo would be much better served by a restoration of all the undermined and disintegrating institutions of control. According to our romantic critics everything would be well if only the genie could be persuaded to retire back into the bottle. The trouble is, though, that he has no intention whatsoever of doing so. Thus, nothing much remains to our romantics except lamenting upon the wickedness of the genie and upon the folly of human beings who let him loose.

4

From "Repressive Tolerance" to the Liberal Advocacy of Repression

When the system fails to cope with the manifestations of dissent, while at the same time it is incapable of dealing with their causal foundations, in such periods of history not only fantasy-figures and remedies appear on the stage but also the "realists" of a repressive rejection of all criticism.

In 1957 a gifted young German writer, Conrad Rheinhold, had to flee the D.D.R. where he used to run a political cabaret in the aftermath of the Twentieth Congress. After he had some experience of life in West Germany, he was asked in an interview published in Der Spiegel,[13] to describe the main difference between his old and new situation. This was his answer: "Im Osten soll das Kabarett die Gesellschaft ändern, darf aber nichts sagen; im Western kann es alles sagen, darf aber nichts ändern." ("In the East political cabaret is supposed to change society, but it is not allowed to say anything; in the West it is allowed to say whatever it pleases but it is not allowed to change anything at all.")

This example illustrates quite well the dilemma of social control. For the other side of the coin of *"repressive* tolerance" is the *"repression* of tolerance". The two together mark the limits of social systems which are incapable of meeting the need for social change in a determinate historical period.

When Marx died in 1883, his death was reported in *The Times* with some delay.[14] And no wonder: for it had to be reported to the London *Times* from *Paris* that Marx had died in *London*. And this, again, illustrates very well our dilemma. For it is easy to be liberal when even a Marx can be totally ignored, since his voice cannot be heard where he lives, thanks to the political and ideological vacuum that surrounds him. But what happens when the political vacuum is displaced by the rising pressure of the ever-increasing social contradictions? Will not, in that case, the frustrations generated by the necessary failure of attending only to the surface manifestations of socioeconomic troubles, instead of tackling their causes, – will not that failure take refuge behind a show of strength, even if this means the violation of the selfsame liberal values in whose name the violation is now committed? The recent case of another young refugee from the D.D.R. – this time not a political cabaret writer but someone deeply concerned about the degradation of politics to the level of cheap cabaret: Rudi Dutschke – suggests a rather disturbing answer to our question.

The issue is not that of "personal aberration" or "political pigheadedness", as some commentators saw it. Unfortunately it is much worse than that: namely an ominous attempt to bring the political organs of control in line with the needs of the present-day articulation of capitalist economy, even if such an adjustment requires a "liberal" transition from "repressive tolerance" to "repressive intolerance". Those who continue to nurse their illusions in these matters should read their allegedly "impartial" daily somewhat more attentively, in order to grasp the carefully woven meaning of passages like this:

The harder the liberal university is pressed, the less comprehensive it can *afford* to be, the more rigorously will it have to draw the line, and the more likely will be the *exclusion of intolerant points of view.* The paradox of the *tolerant society* is that it cannot be defended solely by *tolerant* means just as the *pacific society* cannot be defended solely by peaceful means.[15]

As we can see, the empty myths of "the tolerant society" and "the pacific society" are used to describe the society of *bellum omnium contra omnes,* disregarding the painfully obvious ways in which the "pacific society" of U.S. capitalism demonstrates its true character by saturation bombing, wholesale slaughter and massacres in Vietnam, and by shooting down even its own youth in front of the "liberal university" – in Kent State and elsewhere – when it dares to mount a protest against the unspeakable inhumanities of this "tolerant" and "pacific" society.

Moreover, in such passages of editorial wisdom we can also notice, if we are willing to do so, not only the unintended acknowledgment of the fact that this "liberal" and "tolerant" society will "tolerate" only to the point it can easily *afford* to do so – i.e. only to the point beyond which protest starts to become effective and turns into a genuine social challenge to the perpetuation of the society of repressive tolerance – but also the sophisticated hypocrisy through which the advocacy of *crude* ("rigorous") and *institutionalized intolerance* ("exclusion") succeeds in representing itself as the liberal defence of society against "intolerant points of view".

Similarly, the advocacy of institutionalized intolerance is extended to prescribing "solutions" to Trade Union disputes. Another *Times* leader – significantly entitled: "*A Battle Line at 10 per cent*'[16] – after conceding that "Nobody knows for sure what the mechanism which causes a runaway inflation is", and after murmuring something about the fate of "some sort of authoritarian regime" which befalls the countries with substantial inflation, goes on to advocate blatantly authoritarian measures:

> What can be done to reverse the present inflationary trend? The first and immediate answer is that the country should recognize the justice of *standing firm*. Anyone in present circumstances who asks for more than 10 per cent is joining in a process of self-destruction. Anyone who strikes because he will not accept 15 per cent deserves to be resisted with all the influence of society and *all the power of government*.[17] ... *The first thing to do and the simplest is to start beating strikes*. [!!!] The local authorities should be given *total support* [including troops?] in refusing to make any further offer, *even if the strike lasts for months*.

We can see, then, that the *apparent* concern about the (fictitious) danger of "some sort of authoritarian regime" – which is simply declared to be inevitably linked to major inflations – is only a cover for the real concern about protecting the interests of capital, no matter how grave the political implications of "standing firm" against "strikes lasting for months" might be. To formulate, thus, the highest priorities in terms of "beating the strikes" is and remains *authoritarian*, even if the policy based on such measures is championed in editorial columns capable of assuming liberal positions on peripheral issues.

From the advocacy of institutionalized intolerance, in the form of "beating the strikes with all the power of government", to the legitimation of such practices, through *anti-union laws*, is, of course, only the next logical step. And the record of consensus-politics is particularly telling in this respect.[18] For Mrs. Castle's denunciation of the Tory anti-union bill is not just half-hearted and belated. It also suffers from the memory of its twin brother – the ill-fated Labour bill – for which she could certainly not disclaim maternity.

And when Mrs. Castle writes about *"The Bad Bosses Charter,"*[19] she merely highlights the stubborn illusions of "pragmatic" politicians who, notwithstanding their past experience, still imagine that they will be voted back into office in order to write in the statute books a "Charter for the Good Bosses".

From a socialist point of view, bosses are neither "bad" nor "good". Just *bosses*. And that is bad enough: in fact it could not be worse. This is why it is vital to go beyond the paralysing limits of consensus-politics which refuses to recognize this elementary truth, and makes the people at large pay for the disastrous consequences of its mounting failures.

5

War if the Normal Methods of Expansion Fail

Under the devastating impact of a shrinking rate of profit which must be monopolistically counteracted, the margin of traditional political action has been reduced to slavishly carrying out the dictates arising from the most urgent and immediate demands of capital expansion, even if such operations are invariably misrepresented as "the national interest" by both sides of the "national" consensus.[20] And just how directly policy-making is subordinated to the dictates of monopoly capital – unceremoniously excluding the vast majority of the elected representatives from the determination of all the important matters – is at times revealed in most unexpected ways by such embarrassing events as the headline-catching resignation of supposedly key decision-makers: some members of the most exclusive "inner cabinets" (restricted to a mere handful of ministers) who protest that they had no say in deciding the crucial issues of their own Departments, let alone the national policy as a whole.

Even more revealing is the meteoric rise of the self-appointed representatives of big business and high finance to the top of political decision-making. For – given the vital role assigned to the state in sustaining, with all available means at its disposal, the capitalist system of production, at a time of an already enormous but still extending concentration of capital – so much is at stake that the traditional forms of an indirect (economic) control of policy-making must be abandoned in favour of a *direct* control of the "commanding heights" of politics by the spokesmen of monopoly capital. In contrast to such manifestations of actual economic and political developments which we have all witnessed in the recent past and are still witnessing today, the mythology of realizing socialist ideals by "pragmatically" acquiring control over the "commanding heights of a mixed economy" (Harold Wilson) must sound particularly hollow indeed.

Thus, politics – which is nothing unless it is a conscious application of strategic measures capable of profoundly affecting social development as a whole – is turned into a mere instrument of short-sighted manipulation, completely devoid of any comprehensive plan and design of its own. It is condemned to follow a pattern of belated and short-term reactive moves to the bewildering crisis-events as they necessarily erupt, with increasing frequency, on the socioeconomic basis of self-saturating commodity production and self-stultifying capital accumulation.

The crisis we face, then, is not simply a political crisis, but the general structural crisis of the capitalistic institutions of social control in their entirety. Here the main point is that the institutions of capitalism are inherently violent and aggressive: they are built on the fundamental premise of *"war if the normal methods of expansion fail"*. (Besides, the periodic *destruction* – by whatever means, including the most violent ones – of over-produced capital, is an inherent necessity of the "normal" functioning of this system: the vital condition of its recovery from crisis and depression.) The blind "natural law" of the market mechanism carries with it that the grave social problems necessarily associated with capital production and concentration are never *solved*, only *postponed*, and indeed – since postponement cannot work indefinitely – transferred to the *military* plane. Thus, the "sense" of the hierarchically structured institutions of capitalism is given in its ultimate reference to the violent "fighting out" of the issues, in the international arena. For the socioeconomic units – following the inner logic of their development – grow bigger and bigger, and their problems and contradictions increasingly more intense and grave.

Growth and expansion are immanent necessities of the capitalist system of production and when the local limits are reached there is no way out except by violently readjusting the prevailing relation of forces.

The capitalist system of our times, however, has been decapitated through the removal of its ultimate sanction: an all-out war on its real or potential adversaries. Exporting internal violence is no longer possible on the required massive scale. (Attempts at doing so on a limited scale – e.g. the Vietnam war – not only are no substitutes for the old mechanism but even accelerate the inevitable internal explosions, by aggravating the inner contradictions of the system.) Nor is it possible to get away indefinitely with the ideological mystifications which represented the *internal* challenge of socialism: the only possible solution to the present crisis of social control, as an *external* confrontation, denounced as a "subversion" directed from abroad by a "monolithic" enemy. For the first time in history capitalism is globally confronted with its own problems which cannot be "postponed" much longer, nor indeed can they be transferred to the military plane in order to be "exported" in the form of an all-out war.

Blocking the road of a possible solution to the grave structural crisis of society through a third world war is of

War if the Normal Methods of Expansion Fail 41

an immense significance as far as the future development of capitalism is concerned. The grave implications of this blockage can be grasped by remembering that the "Great Wars" of the past:

1. automatically "de-materialized" the capitalist system of incentives (producing a shift from "economic motives" to "self-denial" and "idealism" so dear to the heart of some recent spokesmen and apologists of the system in trouble), adjusting at the same time, accordingly, the mechanism of "interiorization" through which the continued legitimation of the established order is successfully accomplished;
2. suddenly imposed a radically lower standard of living on the masses of people, who willingly accepted it, given the circumstances of a state of emergency;
3. with equal suddenness radically widened the formerly depressed margin of profit;
4. introduced a vital element of rationalization and co-ordination into the system as a whole (a rationalization, that is, which, thanks to the extraordinary circumstances, did not have to be confined to the narrow limits of all rationalization that directly arises from the sole needs of capital production and expansion); and, last but not least:
5. gave an immense technological boost to the economy as a whole, on a wide front.

Current military demand, however massive, simply cannot be compared to this set of both economic and ideological factors whose removal may well prove too much for the system of world capitalism. The less so since present-day military demand – which is imposed on society under "peace-time" conditions and not under those of a "national emergency" – cannot help intensifying the contradictions of capital production. This fact is powerfully highlighted by the spectacular failures of companies which heavily depend for their survival on mammoth defence contracts (Lockheed and Rolls Royce, for instance).

The issue is, however, far more fundamental than even the most spectacular of business failures could adequately indicate. For it concerns the structure of present-day capitalist production as a whole, and not simply one of its branches. Nor could one reasonably expect the *state* to solve the problem, no matter how much public money is poured down the drain in the course of its revealing *rescue-operations*.

Indeed, it was the tendency of increasing state interventions in economic matters in the service of capital expansion which led to the present state of affairs in the first place. The result of such interventions was not only the cancerous growth of the non-productive branches of industry within the total framework of capital production but – equally important – also the grave distortion of the whole structure of *capitalist cost-accounting* under the impact of contracts carried out with the ideological justification that they were "vital to the national interest". And since present-day capitalism constitutes a closely *interlocking system*, the devastating results of this structural distortion come to the fore in numerous fields and branches of industry, and not only in those which are *directly* involved in the execution of defence contracts. The well known facts that original cost-estimates as a rule madly "escalate", and that the committees set up by governments in order to "scrutinize" them fail to produce results (that is, results other than the white-washing of past operations coupled with generous justifications of future outlays), find their explanation in the immanent necessities of this changed structure of capitalist production and accountancy, with the gravest implications for the future.

Thus, the power of state intervention in the economy – not so long ago still widely believed to be the wonder-drug of all conceivable ills and troubles of the "modern industrial society" – is strictly confined to accelerating the maturation of these contradictions. The larger the doses administered to the convalescing patient, the greater his dependency on the wonder-drug, i.e., the graver the symptoms described above as the structural distortion of the whole system of capitalist cost-accounting: symptoms which menacingly foreshadow the ultimate paralysis and breakdown of the mechanisms of capital production and expansion. And the fact that what is supposed to be the remedy turns out to be a contributory cause of further crisis, clearly demonstrates that we are not concerned here with some "passing dysfunction" but with a fundamental, dynamic contradiction of the *whole structure* of capital production at its *historic phase of decline* and ultimate disintegration.

6

The Emergence of Chronic Unemployment

Equally important is the newly emerging pattern of unemployment. For in recent decades unemployment in the highly developed capitalist countries was largely confined to "pockets of underdevelopment'; and the millions of people affected by it used to be optimistically written off in the grand style of neo-capitalist self-complacency as the "inevitable costs of modernization", without too much – if any – worry about the social-economic repercussions of the trend itself.

Insofar as the prevailing movement was from unskilled to *skilled* jobs, involving large sums of capital outlay in industrial development, the matter could be ignored with relative safety, in the midst of the euphoria of "expansion". Under such circumstances the human misery necessarily associated with all types of unemployment – including the one produced in the interest of "modernization" – could be capitalistically justified in the name of a bright commodity-future for everyone. In those days the unfortunate millions of apathetic, "underprivileged" people could be easily relegated to the periphery of society. Isolated as a social phenomenon from the rest of the "Great Society" of affluence, they were supposed to blame only their own

The Emergence of Chronic Unemployment 45

"uselessness" (want of skill, lack of "drive", etc.) for their predicament, resigned to consume the leftovers of the heavily laden neo-capitalist dinner table magnanimously dished out to them in the form of unemployment "benefits" and unsaleable surplus-food coupons. (We should not forget that in those days some of the most prominent economists were seriously advocating programmes which would have institutionalized – in the name of "technological progress" and "cost-efficiency" – the permanent condemnation of a major proportion of the labour force to the brutally dehumanizing existence of enforced idleness and of a total dependence on "social charity".)

What was systematically ignored, however, was the fact that the trend of capitalist "modernization" and the displacement of large amounts of unskilled labour in preference to a much smaller amount of skilled labour ultimately implied the *reversal* of the trend itself: namely the breakdown of "modernization", coupled with massive unemployment. This fact of the utmost gravity simply *had* to be ignored, in that its recognition is radically incompatible with the continued acceptance of the capitalist perspectives of social control. For the underlying dynamic contradiction which leads to the drastic reversal of the trend is by no means inherent in the *technology* employed, but in the blind subordination of both *labour and technology* to the devastatingly narrow limits of capital as the supreme arbiter of social development and control.

To acknowledge, though, the social embeddedness of the given technology would have amounted to admitting the socioeconomic limitations of the capitalist applications of technology. This is why the apologists of the capitalist relations of production had to theorize about "growth" and "development" and "modernization" *as such*, instead of assessing the sobering *limits* of *capitalist* growth and development. And this is why they had to talk about the "affluent", "modern industrial" – or indeed "post-industrial'(!) – and "consumer" society as such, instead of the artificial, contradictory affluence of *waste-producing commodity society* which relies for its "modern industrial" cycle of reproduction not only on the most cynical manipulation of "consumer-demand" but also on the most callous exploitation of the "have-nots".

Although there is no reason why *in principle* the trend of modernization and the displacement of unskilled by skilled labour should not go on indefinitely, as far as *technology itself* is concerned, there is a very good reason indeed why this trend must be reversed under capitalist relations of production: namely the catastrophically restricting criteria of profitability and expansion of exchange value to which such "modernization" is necessarily subordinated. Thus, the newly emerging pattern of unemployment as a socioeconomic trend is, again, indicative of the deepening structural crisis of present-day capitalism.

In accordance with this trend, the problem is no longer just the plight of unskilled labourers but also that of large numbers of *highly skilled* workers who are now chasing, in addition to the earlier pool of unemployed, the depressingly few available jobs. Also, the trend of "rationalizing" amputation is no longer confined to the "peripheral branches of ageing industry" but embraces some of the *most developed* and modernized sectors of production – from shipbuilding and aviation to electronics, and from engineering to space technology.

Thus, we are no longer concerned with the "normal", and willingly accepted, by-products of "growth and development" but with their driving to a halt; nor indeed with the peripheral problems of "pockets of under-development" but with a fundamental contradiction of the capitalist mode of production as a whole which turns even the latest achievements of "development", "rationalization" and "modernization" into paralysing burdens of chronic underdevelopment. And, most important of all, the human agency which finds itself at the receiving end is no longer the socially powerless, apathetic and fragmented multitude of "underprivileged" people but *all* categories of skilled and unskilled labour: i.e., objectively, the *total labour force* of society.

It goes without saying, we are talking about a major *trend* of social development, and not about some mechanical determinism that announces the immediate collapse of world capitalism. But even though the storehouse of manipulative counter-measures is far from being exhausted, no such measure is capable of suppressing the trend itself in the long run. Whatever might be the rate of success of measures arising from, or compatible with, the basic requirements and limitations of the capitalist mode of production, the crucial fact is and remains that under the present-day circumstances and conditions of capital production the totality of the labour force is becoming involved in an ever-intensifying confrontation with monopoly capital – which carries far-reaching consequences for the development of social consciousness.

7

The Intensification of the Rate of Exploitation

Here we can see, again, the vital importance of blocking the road of possible solutions to the structural crisis of capitalism through the violent displacement of its problems in the form of a new world war. Under the changed circumstances some of the most powerful instruments of mystification – through which capital managed to exercise its paralysing ideological control over labour in the past – become dangerously undermined and tend to collapse altogether. For now the immense tensions generated within the system of capital production cannot be exported on an adequately massive scale at the expense of other countries, and thus the basic social antagonism between capital and labour which lies at the roots of such tensions cannot be sealed down indefinitely: *the contradictions must be fought out at the place where they are actually generated.*

Capital, when it reaches a point of saturation in its own setting and, at the same time, cannot find outlets for further expansion through the vehicle of imperialism and neo-colonialism, has no alternative but to make its own indigenous labour force suffer the grave consequences of the deteriorating rate of profit. Accordingly, the working classes of some of the most developed "post-industrial" societies are getting a foretaste of the real viciousness of "liberal" capital. The interplay of a number of major factors – from the dramatic development of the forces of production to the erection of enormous obstacles to the unhampered international expansion of monopoly capital – have exposed and undermined the mechanism of the traditional "double book-keeping" which in the past enabled capital to conform to the rules of "liberalism" at home while practising and perpetuating the most brutal forms of authoritarianism abroad. Thus, the real nature of the capitalist production relations: the ruthless domination of labour by capital is becoming increasingly more evident as a *global* phenomenon.

Indeed, it could not be otherwise. For so long as the problems of labour are assessed merely in *partial* terms (i.e., as *local* issues of fragmented, stratified and divided groups of workers) they remain a mystery for theory, and nothing but cause for chronic frustration for politically-minded social practice.

The understanding of the development and self-reproduction of the capitalist mode of production is quite impossible without the concept of the *total* social capital, which alone can explain many mysteries of commodity society – from the "average rate of profit" to the laws governing capital expansion and concentration. Similarly, it is quite impossible to understand the manifold and thorny problems of nationally varying as well as socially stratified labour without constantly keeping in mind the necessary framework of a proper assessment: namely the irreconcilable antagonism between *total* social capital and the *totality* of labour.

This fundamental antagonism, it goes without saying, is inevitably modified in accordance with:

a) the local socio-economic circumstances;
b) the respective positions of particular countries in the global framework of capital production; and
c) the relative maturity of the global socio-historical development.

Accordingly, at different periods of time the system as a whole reveals the workings of a complex set of objective differences of interest on *both* sides of the social antagonism. The objective reality of different *rates of exploitation* – both within a given country and in the world system of monopoly capital – is as unquestionable as are the objective differences in the *rates of profit* at any particular time, and the ignorance of such differences can only result in resounding rhetoric, instead of revolutionary strategies. All the same, the reality of the different rates of exploitation and profit does not alter in the least the fundamental law itself: i.e., the growing *equalization* of the differential rates of exploitation as the *global trend* of development of world capital.

To be sure, this law of equalization is a long-term trend as far as the global system of capital is concerned. Nevertheless, the modifications of the system as a whole also appear, inevitably already in the short run, as "disturbances" of a particular economy which happens to be negatively affected by the repercussions of the shifts which necessarily occur within the global framework of total social capital.

The dialectic of such shifts and modifications is extremely complex and cannot be pursued at this place much further. Let it now suffice to stress that "total social capital" should not be confused with "total national capital". When the latter is being affected by a relative weakening of its position within the global system, it will inevitably try to compensate for its losses by increasing its specific rate of exploitation over against the labour force under its direct control – or else its competitive position is further weakened within the global framework of "total social capital". Under the system of capitalist social control there can be no way out from such "short-term disturbances and dysfunctions" other than the intensification of the specific rates of exploitation, which can only lead, both locally and in global terms, to an explosive intensification of the fundamental social antagonism in the long run.

Those who have been talking about the "integration" of the working class – depicting "organized capitalism" as a system which succeeded in radically mastering its social contradictions – have hopelessly misidentified the manipulative success of the differential rates of exploitation (which prevailed in the relatively "disturbance-free" historic phase of post-war reconstruction and expansion) as a basic *structural remedy*.

As a matter of fact, it was nothing of the kind. The ever-increasing frequency with which "temporary disturbances and dysfunctions" appear in all spheres of our social existence, and the utter failure of manipulative measures and instruments devised to cope with them, are clear evidence that the structural crisis of the capitalist mode of social control has assumed all-embracing proportions.

8

Capital's "Correctives" and Socialist Control

The manifest failure of established institutions and their guardians to cope with our problems can only intensify the explosive dangers of a deadlock. And this takes us back to our point of departure: the imperative of an adequate social control which "humanity needs for its sheer survival".

To recognize this need is not the same thing as issuing an invitation to indulge in the production of "practicable" blue-prints of socioeconomic readjustment in the spirit of accomodating liberal meliorism. Those who usually lay down the criterion of "practicability" as the "measure of seriousness" of social criticism, hypocritically hide the fact that their real measure is the capitalist mode of production in terms of which the practicability of all programmes of action is to be evaluated.

Practicable *in relation to what?* – that is the question. For if the criteria of capital production constitute the "neutral" basis of all evaluation, then, of course, no socialist programme can stand the test of this "value-free", "non-ideological" and "objective" approach. This is why Marx himself who insisted that men must change "from top to bottom the conditions of their industrial and political existence, and consequently *their whole manner of being*",[21] must be condemned as a "hopelessly impractical ideologist". For how could men conceivably change from top to bottom the conditions of their existence if conformity to the conditions of capital production remains the necessary premise of all admissible change?

And yet, when the very existence of mankind is at stake, as indeed it happens to be at this juncture of an unprecedented crisis in human history, the only programme which is really practicable – in sharp contrast to the counterproductive practicality of manipulative measures which only aggravate the crisis – is the Marxian programme of radically restructuring, "from top to bottom", the totality of social institutions, the industrial, political and ideological conditions of present-day existence, "the whole manner of being" of men repressed by the alienated and reified conditions of commodity society. Short of the realization of such "unpracticability", there can be no way out from the ever-deepening crisis of human existence.

The demand for "practicable" blue-prints is the manifestation of a desire to integrate the "constructive" elements of social criticism; a desire coupled with the determination to devise ruthlessly effective counter-measures against those elements which resist integration, and therefore *a priori* defined as "destructive". But even if this were not so: truly adequate programmes and instruments of socio-political action can only be elaborated by critical and self-critical social practice itself, in the course of its actual development.

Thus, the socialist institutions of social control cannot define themselves *in detail* prior to their practical articulation. At this point of historic transition the relevant questions concern their general character and direction: determined, in the first place, by the prevailing mode and institutions of control to which they have to constitute a radical alternative. Accordingly, the central characteristics of the new mode of social control can be concretely identified – to a degree to which this is necessary for the elaboration and implementation of flexible socialist strategies – through the grasp of the basic functions and inherent contradictions of the disintegrating system of social control.[22]

Here we must confine ourselves to mentioning only the most important points – among them the relationship between politics and economics in the first place. As is well known, Marx's bourgeois critics never ceased to accuse him of "economic determinism". Nothing could be, however, further removed from the truth. For the Marxian programme is formulated precisely as the *emancipation* of human action from the power of relentless economic determinations.

When Marx demonstrated that the brute force of economic determinism, set into motion by the dehumanizing necessities of capital production, rules over all aspects of human life, demonstrating at the same time the inherently *historical* – i.e. necessarily *transient* – character of the prevailing mode of production, he touched a sore point of bourgeois ideology: the hollowness of its metaphysical belief in the "natural law" of permanence of the given production relations. And by revealing the inherent contradictions of this mode of production, he demonstrated the necessary *breakdown* of its objective economic determinism. Such a breakdown, however, had to consummate itself by extending the power of capital to its extreme limits, submitting absolutely everything – including the supposedly autonomous power of political decision-making – to its own mechanism of strict control.

Ironically, though, when this is accomplished (as a result of an increasingly bigger appetite for "correctives" devised to safeguard the unhampered expansion of the power of capital), monopoly capital is compelled to assume direct control also over areas which it is structurally incapable of controlling. Thus, beyond a certain point, the more it controls (directly), the less it controls (effectively), undermining and eventually destroying even the mechanisms of "correctives". The complete and by now overt subordination of politics to the most immediate dictates of capital-producing economic determinism is a vital aspect of this problematic. This is why the road to the establishment of the new institutions of social control must lead through a *radical emancipation of politics from the power of capital.*

Another basic contradiction of the capitalist system of control is that it cannot separate "advance" from *destruction*, nor "progress" from *waste* – however catastrophic the results. The more it unlocks the powers of productivity, the more it must unleash the powers of destruction; and the more it extends the volume of production, the more it must bury everything under mountains of suffocating waste. The concept of *economy* is radically incompatible with the "economy" of capital production which, of necessity, adds insult to injury by first using up with rapacious wastefulness the *limited resources* of our planet, and then further aggravates the outcome by *polluting and poisoning* the human environment with its mass-produced waste and effluence.

Ironically, though, again, the system breaks down at the point of its supreme power; for its maximum extension inevitably generates the vital need for restraint and conscious control with which capital production is structurally incompatible. Thus, the establishment of the new mode of social control is inseparable from the realization of the principles of a *socialist economy* which centre on a *meaningful economy of productive activity:* the pivotal point of a rich human fulfilment in a society emancipated from the alienated and reified institutions of control.

And the final point to stress is the necessarily global determination of the alternative system of social control, in confrontation with the global system of capital as a mode of control. In the world as it has been – and is still being – transformed by the immense power of capital, the social institutions constitute a closely interlocking system. Thus, there is no hope for *isolated partial* successes, only for *global* ones – however paradoxical this might sound. Accordingly, the crucial criterion for the assessment of partial measures is whether or not they are capable of functioning as "Archimedean points". i.e. as *strategic levers* for a radical restructuring of the global system of social control. This is why Marx spoke of the vital necessity of changing, "from top to bottom", the conditions of existence *as a whole,* short of which all efforts directed at a socialist emancipation of mankind are doomed to failure. Such a programme, it goes without saying, embraces the "micro-structures" (like the family) just as much as the most comprehensive institutions (the "macro-structures") of political and economic life. Indeed, as Marx had suggested, nothing less than a radical transformation of our "whole manner of being" can produce an adequate system of social control.

Its establishment will, no doubt, take time and will require the most active involvement of the whole community of producers, activating the repressed creative energies of the various social groups over matters incomparably greater in importance than deciding the colour of local lamp-posts to which their "power of decision-making" is confined today.

The establishment of this social control will, equally, require the conscious cultivation – not in isolated individuals but in the whole community of producers, to whatever walk of life they may belong – of an uncompromising critical awareness, coupled with an intense commitment to the values of a socialist humanity, which guided the work of Isaac Deutscher to a rich fulfilment.

Thus, our memorial is not a ritual remembrance of the past but a persistent challenge to face up to the demands inherent in our own share of a shared task.

It is in this spirit that I wish to dedicate my lecture to the memory of Isaac Deutscher.

Appendix

Structural Crisis Needs Structural Change[23]

When stressing the need for a radical structural change it must be made clear right from the beginning that this is not a call for an unrealizable utopia. On the contrary, the primary defining characteristic of modern utopian theories was precisely the projection that their intended improvement in the conditions of the workers' lives could be achieved well within the *existing structural framework* of the criticized societies. Thus Robert Owen of New Lanark, for instance, who had an ultimately untenable business partnership with the utilitarian liberal philosopher Jeremy Bentham, attempted the general realization of his enlightened social and educational reforms in that spirit. He was asking for the *impossible*. As we also know, the high-sounding "utilitarian" moral principle of "the greatest good for the greatest number" came to nothing since its Benthamite advocacy. The problem for us is that without a proper assessment of the nature of the economic and social crisis of our time — which by now cannot be denied by the defenders of the capitalist order even if they reject the need for a major change — the likelihood of success in this respect is negligible. The demise of the "Welfare State" even in the mere handful of the privileged countries where it has been once instituted offers a sobering lesson on this score.

Let me start by quoting a recent article by the editors of the authoritative daily newspaper of the international bourgeoisie, *The Financial Times*. Talking about the dangerous financial crisis — acknowledged now by the editors themselves to be dangerous — they end their article with these words: "Both sides [the U.S. Democrats and the Republicans] are to blame for a vacuum of leadership and responsible deliberation. It is a serious failure of governance and more dangerous than Washington believes."[24] This is all that we get as editorial wisdom about the substantive issue of "sovereign indebtedness" and mounting budget deficits. What makes the *Financial Times* editorial even more vacuous than the "vacuum of leadership" deplored by the journal is the sonorous subtitle of this article: "*Washington must stop posturing and start governing.*" As if editorials like this could amount to more than posturing in the name of "governing"! For the grave issue at stake is the catastrophic indebtedness of the "power-house" of global capitalism, the United States of America, where the government's debt alone (without adding corporate and private individual indebtedness) is counted already in well above *14 trillion dollars* (in June 2011) — flashed up in large illuminated numbers on the façade of a New York public building, indicating the irresistible trend of rising debt.

The point I wish to stress is that the crisis we have to face is a profound and deepening structural crisis which needs the adoption of far-reaching structural remedies in order to achieve a sustainable solution. It must also be stressed that the structural crisis of our time did not originate in 2007, with the "bursting of the US housing bubble," but at least four decades earlier. I spoke about it in such terms way back in 1967, well before the May 1968 explosion in France,[25] and I wrote in 1971, in the Preface to the Third Edition of *Marx's Theory of Alienation*, that the unfolding events and developments "dramatically underlined the intensification of the global structural crisis of capital."

In this respect it is necessary to clarify the relevant differences between types or modalities of crisis. It is not a matter of indifference whether a crisis in the social sphere can be considered a *periodic/conjunctural crisis*, or something much more fundamental than that. For, obviously, the way of dealing with a fundamental structural crisis cannot be conceptualized in terms of the categories of periodic or conjunctural crises. The crucial difference between the two sharply contrasting types of crises is that the periodic or conjunctural crises unfold and are more or less successfully resolved within the established framework, whereas the fundamental crisis affects that framework itself in its entirety.

In general terms, this distinction is not simply a question of the apparent severity of the contrasting types of crises. For a periodic or conjunctural crisis can be dramatically severe — as the "Great World Economic Crisis of 1929–1933" happened to be — yet capable of a solution within the parameters of the given system. And in the same way, but in the opposite sense, the "non-explosive" character of a prolonged structural crisis, in contrast to the "great thunderstorms" (in Marx's words) through which periodic conjunctural crises can discharge and resolve themselves, may lead to fundamentally misconceived strategies, as a result of the misinterpretation of the absence of "thunderstorms"; as if their absence was the overwhelming evidence for the indefinite stability of "organized capitalism" and of the "integration of the working class."

It cannot be stressed enough that the crisis in our time

is not intelligible without being referred to the broad overall social framework. This means that in order to clarify the nature of the persistent and deepening crisis all over the world today we must focus attention on the crisis of the capital system in its entirety. For the crisis of capital we are experiencing is an all-embracing structural crisis.

Let us see, summed up as briefly as possible, the defining characteristics of the structural crisis we are concerned with.

The *historical* novelty of today's crisis is manifest under four main aspects:

1. its *character* is *universal,* rather than restricted to one particular sphere (e.g., financial, or commercial, or affecting this or that particular branch of production, or applying to this rather than that type of labor, with its specific range of skills and degrees of productivity, etc.);
2. its *scope* is truly *global* (in the most threateningly literal sense of the term), rather than confined to a particular set of countries (as all major crises have been in the past);
3. its *time scale* is extended, continuous — if you like: *permanent* — rather than limited and *cyclic,* as all former crises of capital happened to be;
4. its *mode* of unfolding might be called *creeping* — in contrast to the more spectacular and dramatic eruptions and collapses of the past — while adding the proviso that even the most vehement or violent convulsions cannot be excluded as far as the future is concerned: i.e., when the complex machinery now actively engaged in "crisis-management" and in the more or less temporary "displacement" of the growing contradictions runs out of steam.

62 The Necessity of Social Control

[Here] it is necessary to make some general points about the criteria of a structural crisis, as well as about the forms in which its solution may be envisaged.

To put it in the simplest and most general terms, a structural crisis affects the *totality* of a social complex, in all its relations with its constituent parts or sub-complexes, as well as with other complexes to which it is linked. By contrast, a non-structural crisis affects only some parts of the complex in question, and thus no matter how severe it might be with regard to the affected parts, it cannot endanger the continued survival of the overall structure.

Accordingly, the displacement of contradictions is feasible only while the crisis is partial, relative and internally manageable by the system, requiring no more than shifts — even if major ones — *within* the relatively autonomous system itself. By the same token, a structural crisis calls into question the very existence of the overall complex concerned, postulating its transcendence and replacement by some alternative complex.

The same contrast may be expressed in terms of the limits any particular social complex happens to have in its immediacy, at any given time, as compared to those beyond which it cannot conceivably go. Thus, a structural crisis is not concerned with the *immediae* limits but with the *ultimate* limits of a global structure.[26]

Thus, in a fairly obvious sense, nothing could be more serious than the structural crisis of capital's mode of social metabolic reproduction which defines the ultimate limits of the established order. But even though profoundly serious in its all-important general parameters, on the face of it the structural crisis may not appear to be of such a deciding importance when compared to the dramatic vicissitudes of a major conjunctural crisis. For the "thunderstorms" through which the conjunctural crises discharge themselves are rather paradoxical in the sense that in their mode of unfolding they not only discharge (and impose) but also resolve themselves, to the degree to which that is feasible under the circumstances. This they can do precisely because of their partial character which does not call into question the ultimate limits of the established global structure. At the same time, however (and for the same reason), they can only "resolve" the underlying deep-seated structural problems — which necessarily reassert themselves again and again in the form of the specific conjunctural crises — in a strictly partial and temporally also most limited way. Until, that is, the next conjunctural crisis appears on society's horizon.

By contrast, in view of the inescapably complex and prolonged nature of the structural crisis, unfolding in historical time in an *epochal* and not episodic/instantaneous sense, it is the cumulative interrelationship of the whole that decides the issue, even under the false appearance of "normality." This is because in the structural crisis everything is at stake, involving the all-embracing ultimate limits of the given order of which there cannot possibly be a "symbolic/paradigmatic" particular instance. Without understanding the overall systemic connections and implications of the particular events and developments we lose sight of the really significant changes and of the corresponding levers of potential strategic intervention to positively affect them, in the interest of the necessary systemic transformation. Our social responsibility therefore calls for an uncompromising critical awareness of the emerging cumulative interrelationship, instead of looking for comforting reassurances in the world of illusory normality until the house collapses over our head.

It is necessary to underline here that for nearly three decades after the Second World War the successful economic expansion in the dominant capitalist countries generated the illusion even among some major intellectuals of the left that the historic phase of "crisis capitalism" had been overcome, leaving its place to what they called "advanced organized capitalism."

I want to illustrate this problem by quoting some passages from the work of one of the greatest militant intellectuals of the twentieth century, Jean-Paul Sartre, for whom, as you may well know from my book on Sartre, I have the highest regard. However, the fact is that the adoption of the notion that by overcoming "crisis capitalism" the established order turned itself into "advanced capitalism" created some major dilemmas for Sartre. This is all the more significant because no one can deny Sartre's fully committed search for a viable emancipatory solution and his great personal integrity.

In relation to our problem we have to recall that in the important interview given to the Italian Manifesto group — after outlining his conception of the insuperably negative implications of his own explanatory category of the unavoidably detrimental *institutionalization* of what he called the "fused group" in his *Critique of Dialectical Reason* — he had to come to the painful conclusion that:

> While I recognize the need of an *organization*, I must confess that I don't see how the problems which confront *any stabilized structure* could be resolved.[27]

Here the difficulty is that the terms of Sartre's social analysis are set up in such a way that the various factors and correlations that in reality belong together, constituting different facets of fundamentally the *same societal complex*, are depicted by him in the form of most problematical dichotomies and oppositions, generating thereby insoluble dilemmas and an unavoidable defeat for the emancipatory social forces. This is clearly shown by the exchange between the Manifesto group and Sartre:

Manifesto: On what precise bases can one prepare a revolutionary alternative?

Sartre: I repeat, more on the basis of *"alienation"* than on *"needs."* In short on the reconstruction of the *individual* and of *freedom* — the need for which is so pressing that even the most refined *techniques of integration* cannot afford to discount it.[28]

Thus Sartre in this way, in his strategic assessment of how to overcome the oppressive character of capitalist reality, sets up a totally untenable opposition between the workers" "alienation" and their allegedly satisfied "needs," thereby making it all the more difficult to envisage a practically feasible positive outcome. And here the problem is not simply that he grants far too much credibility to the fashionable but extremely superficial sociological explanation of the so-called *"refined techniques of integration"* in relation to the workers. Unfortunately it is much more serious than that.

Indeed the really disturbing problem at stake is the evaluation of the viability of *"advanced capitalism"* itself and the associated postulate of working class "integration" which Sartre happens to share at the time to a large extent with Herbert Marcuse. For in actuality the truth of the matter is that in contrast to the undoubtedly feasible integration of some particular workers into the capitalist order, the *class* of labor — the structural antagonist of capital, representing the only *historically sustainable hegemonic alternative* to the capital system — cannot be integrated into capital's alienating and exploitative framework of societal reproduction. What makes that impossible is the underlying *structural antagonism* between capital and labor, emanating with insurmountable necessity from the class reality of antagonistic domination and subordination.

In this discourse even the minimal plausibility of the Marcuse/Sartre type of false alternative between continuing alienation and "satisfied need" is "established" on the basis of the derailing compartmentalization of capital's suicidally untenable globally entrenched structural interdeterminations upon which in fact the elementary systemic viability of capital's one and only ruling societal metabolic order is necessarily premised. Thus it is extremely problematical to separate "advanced capitalism" from the so-called "marginal zones" and from the "third world." As if the reproductive order of the postulated "advanced capitalism" could sustain itself for *any length of time*, let alone *indefinitely* in the future, without the ongoing exploitation of the misconceived "marginal zones" and the imperialistically dominated "third world"!

It is necessary to quote here the relevant passage in which these problems are spelled out by Sartre. The revealing Manifesto interview passage in question reads as follows:

Advanced capitalism, in relation to its awareness of its own condition, and despite the enormous disparities in the distribution of income, manages to satisfy the elementary needs of the majority of the working class — there remains of course the *marginal zones*, 15 percent of workers in the United States, the blacks and the immigrants; there remain the elderly; there remains, on the global scale, the *third world*. But capitalism satisfies certain primary needs, and also satisfies certain needs which it has artificially created: for instance the *need of a car*. It is this situation which has caused me to revise my "theory of needs," since these needs are no longer, in a situation of *advanced capitalism*, in systematic opposition to the system. On the contrary, they partly become, under the control of that system, an instrument of *integration of the proletariat* into certain processes engendered and directed by profit. The worker exhausts himself in producing a car and in earning enough to buy one; this *acquisition* gives him the *impression* of having satisfied a "*need*." The system which exploits him provides him simultaneously with a goal and with the possibility of reaching it. The consciousness of the intolerable character of the system must therefore no longer be sought in the impossibility of satisfying elementary needs but, above all else, in the consciousness of alienation — in other words, in the fact that *this life is not worth living and has no meaning*, that this mechanism is a deceptive mechanism, that these needs are artificially created, that they are false, that they are exhausting and only serve profit. But to unite the class on this basis is even *more difficult*.[29]

If we accept at face value this characterization of the "advanced capitalist" order, in that case the task of producing emancipatory consciousness is not only *"more difficult"* but quite *impossible*. But the dubious ground on which we can reach such *a prioristic* imperatival and pessimistic/self-defeating conclusion — prescribing from the height of the intellectual's "new theory of needs" the abandonment by the workers of their "acquisitive artificial needs," instantiated by the motor car, and their replacement by the thoroughly abstract postulate which posits for them that *"this life is not worth living and has no meaning"* (a noble but rather abstract imperatival postulate effectively contradicted in reality by the tangible need of the members of the working class for securing the conditions of their economically sustainable existence) — is both the *acceptance* of a set of totally untenable *assertions* and the equally untenable *omission* of some vital determining features of the actually existing capital system in its historically irreversible *structural crisis*.

For a start, to talk about *"advanced* capitalism" — when the capital system as a mode of social metabolic reproduction finds itself in its *descending phase of historical development*, and therefore is only *capitalistically* advanced but in no other sense at all, thereby capable of sustaining itself only in an ever more *destructive* and therefore ultimately also *self-destructive* way — is extremely problematical. Another assertion: the characterization of the *overwhelming majority of humankind* — in the category of poverty, including the "blacks and the immigrants," the "elderly," and, "on the global scale, the third world" — as belonging to the *"marginal zones"* (in affinity with Marcuse's "outsiders"), is no less untenable. For in reality it is the "advanced capitalist world" that constitutes the long term totally unsustainable privileged *margin* of the overall system, with its ruthless "elementary need-denial" to the greater part of the world, and not what is described by Sartre in his Manifesto interview as the "marginal zones." Even with regard to the United States of America the margin of poverty is greatly underrated, at merely 15 per cent. Besides, the characterization of the workers' motor cars as nothing more than purely "artificial needs" which "only serve profit" could not be more one-sided. For, in contrast to many intellectuals, not even the relatively well-off particular workers, let alone the members of the class of labor as a whole, have the luxury of finding their place of work next door to their bedroom.

At the same time, on the side of the astonishing omissions, some of the gravest structural contradictions and failures are missing from Sartre's depiction of "advanced capitalism," virtually emptying the whole concept of meaning. In this sense one of the most important substantive needs without which no society — past, present, or future — could survive, is the need for work. Both for the productively active individuals — embracing all of them in a fully emancipated social order — and for society in general in its historically sustainable relationship to nature. The necessary failure to solve this fundamental structural problem, affecting *all* categories of work not only in the "third world" but even in the most privileged countries of "advanced capitalism," with its perilously rising unemployment, constitutes one of the *absolute limits* of the capital system in its entirety.

Another grave problem which underscores the present and future historical unviability of capital is the calamitous shift toward the *parasitic sectors* of the economy — like the crisis-producing adventurist speculation which plagues (as a matter of *objective necessity,* often misrepresented as systemically irrelevant *personal* failure) the financial sector and the institutionalized/legally buttressed *fraudulence* closely associated with it — in contradistinction to the productive branches of socioeconomic life required for the satisfaction of genuine human need. This is a shift that stands in menacingly sharp contrast to the ascending phase of capital's historic development, when the prodigious systemic expansionary dynamism (including the industrial revolution) was overwhelmingly due to socially viable and further enhanceable productive achievements. We have to add to all this the *massively wasteful* economic burdens imposed on society in an authoritarian way by the state and the military/industrial complex — with the permanent arms industry and the corresponding wars — as an integral part of the perverse "economic growth" of "advanced organized capitalism."

And to mention just one more of the catastrophic implications of "advanced" capital's systemic development, we must bear in mind the prohibitively wasteful global ecological encroachment of our no longer tenable mode of social metabolic reproduction on the finite planetary world,[30] with its rapacious exploitation of the non-renewable material resources and the increasingly more dangerous destruction of nature. Saying this is not "being wise after the event." I wrote in the same period when Sartre

gave his Manifesto interview that:
> Another basic contradiction of the capitalist system of control is that it cannot separate "advance" from *destruction*, nor "progress" from *waste* — however catastrophic the results. The more it unlocks the powers of productivity, the more it must unleash the powers of destruction; and the more it extends the volume of production, the more it must bury everything under mountains of suffocating waste. The concept of *economy* is radically incompatible with the "economy" of capital production which, of necessity, adds insult to injury by first using up with rapacious wastefulness the *limited resources* of our planet, and then further aggravates the outcome by *polluting and poisoning* the human environment with its mass-produced waste and effluence.[31]

Thus the problematical *assertions* and the seminally important *omissions* of Sartre's characterization of "advanced capitalism" greatly weaken the power of negation of his emancipatory discourse. His dichotomous principle which repeatedly asserts the "irreducibility of the cultural order to the natural order" is always on the look out for finding solutions in terms of the "cultural order," at the level of the individuals' consciousness, through the committed intellectual's "*work of consciousness upon consciousness.*" He appeals to the idea that the required solution lies in increasing the "consciousness of alienation" — that is, in terms of his "cultural order" — while at the same time discarding the viability of grounding the revolutionary strategy on *need* belonging to the "natural order." Material need which is said to be already satisfied for the majority of the workers and which in any case constitutes a "deceptive and false mechanism" and an "instrument of integration of the proletariat."

To be sure, Sartre is deeply concerned with the challenge

of addressing the issue of how to increase "the consciousness of the intolerable character of the system." But, as a matter of unavoidable consideration, the leverage itself indicated as the vital condition of success — the power of the "consciousness of alienation" stressed by Sartre — would itself badly need some objective underpinning. Otherwise, the idea (even setting aside the indicated leverage's weakness of self-referential circularity) that it somehow "*can* prevail over against the intolerable character of the system" is bound to be dismissed as a noble but ineffective *cultural* advocacy. That this is problematic even in Sartre's own terms of reference is indicated by his rather pessimistic words wherein he shows that the need is to defeat the materially and culturally destructive and structurally entrenched reality of "this miserable ensemble which is our planet," with its "horrible, ugly, bad determinations, without hope."

Accordingly, the primary question concerns the — demonstrability or not — of the *objectively intolerable* character of the system itself. For if the demonstrable intolerability of the system is missing in *substantive* terms, as proclaimed by the notion of "advanced capitalism's ability to satisfy material needs" except in the "marginal zones," then the *"long and patient labor in the construction of consciousness"*[32] advocated by Sartre remains well-nigh impossible. It is that objective grounding that needs to be (and in actuality can be) established in its own comprehensive terms of reference, requiring the radical demystification of the increasing destructiveness of "advanced capitalism." The *"consciousness* of the intolerable character of the system" can only be built on that *objective grounding* — which includes the suffering caused by "advanced" capital's failure to satisfy even the elementary need for food not only in "marginal zones" but for countless millions, as clearly evidenced by food riots in many countries — so as to be able to overcome the postulated dichotomy between the cultural order and the natural order. In its *ascending* phase the capital system was successfully asserting its productive accomplishments on the basis of its internal expansionary dynamism — still without the imperative of a *monopolistic/imperialist* drive of the capitalistically most advanced countries for militarily secured world domination. Yet, through the historically irreversible circumstance of entering the *productively descending* phase, the capital system had become inseparable from an ever-intensifying need for the militaristic/monopolistic extension and overstretch of its structural framework, tending in due course on the internal productive plane toward the establishment and the criminally wasteful operation of a "permanent arms industry," together with the wars necessarily associated with it.

In fact well before the outbreak of the First World War Rosa Luxemburg clearly identified the nature of this fateful monopolistic/imperialist development on the destructively productive plane by writing in her book on *The Accumulation of Capital* about the role of massive militarist production that: "Capital itself ultimately controls this automatic and rhythmic movement of militarist production through the legislature and a press whose function is to mould so-called 'public opinion.' That is why this particular province of capitalist accumulation at first seems capable of infinite expansion."[33]

In another respect, the increasingly wasteful utilization of energy and vital material strategic resources carried with it not only the ever more destructive articulation of capital's self-assertive structural determinations on the (by legislatively manipulated "public opinion" never even questioned, let alone properly regulated) military plane but also with regard to the increasingly destructive encroachment of capital-expansion on nature. Ironically but by no means surprisingly, this turn of *regressive historical development* of the capital system as such also carried with it some bitterly negative consequences for the international organization of labor.

Indeed, this new articulation of the capital system in the last third of the nineteenth century, with its monopolistic imperialist phase inseparable from its fully extended global ascendancy, opened up a new modality of (most antagonistic and ultimately untenable) expansionary dynamism at the overwhelming benefit of a mere handful of privileged imperialist countries, postponing thereby the ."moment of truth" that goes with the system's irrepressible *structural crisis* in our own time. This type of monopolistic imperialist development inevitably gave a major boost to the possibility of militaristic capital-expansion and accumulation, no matter how great a price had to be paid in due course for the ever-intensifying destructiveness of the new expansionary dynamism. Indeed, the militarily underpinned monopolistic dynamism had to assume the form of even two devastating *global wars*, as well as the total annihilation of humankind implicit in a potential *Third World War*, in addition to the ongoing perilous destruction of nature that became evident in the second half of the twentieth century.

In our time we are experiencing the deepening structural crisis of the capital system. Its destructiveness is visible everywhere, and it shows no signs of diminishing. With regard to the future it is crucial how we conceptualize the nature of the crisis in order to envisage its solution. For the same reason it is also necessary to re-examine some of the major solutions projected in the past. Here it is not possible to do more than to mention, with stenographic brevity, the contrasting approaches which have been offered, indicating at the same time what happened to them in actuality.

First, we have to remember that it was to his merit that liberal philosopher John Stuart Mill considered how problematical endless capitalist growth might be, suggesting as the solution of this problem the "stationary state of the economy." Naturally, such a "stationary state" under the capital system could be nothing more than wishful thinking, because it is totally incompatible with the imperative of capital-expansion and accumulation. Even today, when so much destructiveness is caused by unqualified growth and the most wasteful allocation of our vital energy and strategic material resources, the mythology of growth is constantly reasserted, coupled with the wishful projection of "reducing our carbon imprint" by the year 2050, while in reality moving in the opposite direction. Thus the reality of liberalism turned out to be the aggressive destructiveness of neo-liberalism.

Similar fate affected the social democratic perspective. Marx clearly formulated his warnings about this danger in his *Critique of the Gotha Programme*, but they were totally ignored. Here, too, the contradiction between the promised Bernsteinian "evolutionary socialism" and its realization everywhere turned out to be striking. Not only in virtue of the capitulation of social-democratic parties and governments to the lure of imperialist wars but also through the transformation of social democracy in general — including British "New Labour" — into more or less open versions of neo-liberalism, abandoning not only the "road of evolutionary socialism" but even the once promised implementation of significant social reform.

Moreover, a much propagandized solution to the gruesome inequalities of the capital system was the promised worldwide diffusion of the "Welfare State" after the Second World War. However, the prosaic reality of this claimed historic achievement turned out to be not only the utter failure to institute the Welfare State in any part of the so-called "Third World," but the ongoing liquidation of the relative achievements of the postwar Welfare State — in the field of social security, health care, and education — even in the handful of privileged capitalist countries where they were once instituted.

And of course we cannot disregard the promise to realize the highest phase of socialism (by Stalin and others) through the overthrow and abolition of capitalism. For, tragically, seven decades after the October Revolution the reality turned out to be the restoration of capitalism in a regressive neoliberal form in the countries of the former Soviet Union and Eastern Europe.

The common denominator of all of these failed attempts — despite some of their major differences — is that they all tried to accomplish their objectives within the structural framework of the established social metabolic order. However, as painful historical experience teaches us, our problem is not simply "the overthrow of capitalism." For even to the extent to which that objective can be accomplished, it is bound to be only a very unstable achievement, because whatever can be *overthrown* can be also *restored*. The real — and much more difficult — issue is the necessity of *radical structural change*.

The tangible meaning of such *structural change* is the *complete eradication of capital itself from the social metabolic process*. In other words, the eradication of capital from the metabolic process of societal reproduction.

Capital itself is an all-embracing mode of *control;* which means that it either controls everything or it implodes as a system of societal reproductive control. Consequently, capital as such cannot be controlled in some of its aspects while leaving the rest at its place. All attempted measures and modalities of "controlling" capital's various functions on a lasting basis have failed in the past. In view of its *structurally entrenched uncontrollability* — which means that there is no conceivable leverage *within the structural framework of the capital system* through which the system itself could be brought under lasting control — capital must be completely *eradicated*. This is the *central meaning* of Marx's lifework.

In our time the question of control — through the institution of *structural change* in response to our deepening structural crisis — is becoming urgent not only in the financial sector, due to the wasted trillions of dollars, but everywhere. The leading capitalist financial journals complain that "China is sitting on three trillion dollars of cash," wishfully projecting again solutions through the "better use of that money." But the sobering truth is that the total worsening indebtedness of capitalism amounts to ten times more than China's "unused dollars." Besides, even if the huge current indebtedness could be eliminated somehow, although no one can say how, the real question would remain: How was it generated in the first place, and how can be made sure that it is not generated again in the future? This is why the productive dimension of the system — namely the capital relation itself — is what must be fundamentally changed in order to overcome the *structural crisis* through the appropriate *structural change*.

The dramatic financial crisis which we experienced in the last three years is only one aspect of the capital system's three-pronged destructiveness:

1. in the military field, with capital's interminable wars since the onset of monopolistic imperialism in the final decades of the nineteenth century, and its ever

more devastating weapons of mass destruction in the last sixty years;
2. in the intensification through capital's obvious destructive impact on ecology directly affecting and endangering by now the elementary natural foundation of human existence itself; and
3. in the domain of material production an ever-increasing waste, due to the advancement of "destructive production" in place of the once eulogized "creative" or "productive destruction."

These are the grave systemic problems of our *structural crisis* which can only be solved by a comprehensive *structural change*.

In conclusion, let me quote the last few lines of *The Dialectic of Structure and History*. They read as follows:

> Naturally, historical dialectic in the abstract cannot offer any guarantee for a positive outcome. To expect that would mean renouncing our role in developing social consciousness, which is integral to the historical dialectic. Radicalizing social consciousness in an emancipatory spirit is what we need for the future, and we need it more than ever before.[34]

References

* *Marx's Theory of Alienation* by István Mészáros was awarded the Isaac Deutscher Memorial Prize in 1970. The first Isaac Deutscher Memorial lecture, on The Necessity of Social Control, was delivered at the London School of Economics and Political Science on 26 January 1971. Published as a separate volume, under the same title, by The Merlin Press, London, 1971.
1. Isaac Deutscher, *The Unfinished Revolution*, Oxford University Press, 1967, pp. 110-4.
2. W.W. Rostow, *The Stages of Economic Growth: A Non-Communist Manifesto*, Cambridge University Press, 1960, pp. 157-64.
3. People often forget that President Kennedy was directly responsible for the escalating U.S. involvement in Vietnam, inaugurating a whole series of disastrous policies conceived on the basis of "theories" like the one quoted above.
4. Here is a graphic example of tautological apologetics based on a retrospective reconstruction of the past in the key of an idealized present of U.S. capitalism:
   The relative inter-war stagnation in Western Europe was due not to long-run diminishing return but to the failure of Western Europe to create a setting in which its national societies moved promptly into the age of high mass-consumption, yielding new leading sectors. And this failure, in turn, was due mainly to a failure to create initial full

employment in the post-1920 setting of the terms of trade. Similarly the protracted depression of the United States in the 1930s was due not to long-run diminishing returns, but to a failure to create an initial renewed setting of full employment, through public policy, which would have permitted the new leading sectors of suburban housing, the diffusion of automobiles, durable consumers" goods and services to roll forward beyond 1929. (Rostow, op. cit., p. 155.) Thus, "failures" (crises and recessions) are explained by the "failure" to realize the conditions which "would have permitted" the avoidance of those unfortunate "failures", by producing the present-day pattern of capitalist "high-consumption" which is, of course, the non plus ultra of everything. How those unfortunate, failure-explanatory failures came into being, we are not told. Since, however, the point of the whole exercise is the propagation of Rostow's "objective" and "non-parochial" Non-Communist Manifesto as the ultimate salvation of U.S. dominated world capitalism, by implication we can take it that the "failures" in question must have been due to the absence of this retrospective-tautological economico-political wisdom. By what "failures" he would explain today's rising unemployment and the associated symptoms of serious structural disturbances in the U.S. as well as in other parts of the capitalist world of "high mass-consumption", "suburban housing", etc., must remain, unfortunately, a mystery to us, since there are no "new leading sectors" in sight whose creation "would have permitted" the avoidance of present-day failures.
5. Rostow, op. cit., p. 163.
6. Marx and Engels, *The German Ideology*, pp. 55-6.
7. Ibid., p. 56.
8. I have discussed several related problems in "Contingent and Necessary Class Consciousness", my contribution to *Aspects of History and Class Consciousness*, Essays by Tom Bottomore, David Daiches, Lucien Goldmann, Arnold Hauser, E.J. Hobsbawm, István Mészáros, Ralph Miliband, Rudolf Schlesinger, Anthony Thorlby, Edited by I. Mészáros,

80 *The Necessity of Social Control*

      Routledge & Kegan Paul, London, 1971; reprinted in István Mészáros, *Philosophy, Ideology and Social Science*, Harvester Press, Brighton, 1986, pp. 57-104.
9. See Marx, *Grundrisse der Kritik der politischen Ökonomie*, Berlin, 1953, pp. 593-4.
10. This is how the "Voice of America" introduces its programme of interviews with intellectuals on "Man and his Survival":

    The order of importance of great tasks has changed. Today no longer the clash of national interests, or the struggle for political power occupy the first place; nor indeed the elimination of social injustice. The outstanding issue by now is whether or not mankind will succeed in securing the conditions of its survival in a world it has transformed. ... No wonder that the President of the United States has dedicated two thirds of his latest "State of the Union" message to the question of how to rehabilitate the environment from pollution. What happens, though, if man, instead of thinking about his own survival, wastes his energies in fighting for the relative truth of various ideologies and social-political systems? What are the first steps mankind ought to take in order to reform itself and the world?

    Further comment is quite unnecessary, thanks to the transparency of these lines.
11. A capability so far very effectively paralysed by the guardians of the ruling order. For a penetrating analysis of the dynamic potentialities of the "mass media", see Hans Magnus Enzensberger: "Constituents of a Theory of the Media", *New Left Review*, No. 64 (November-December 1970), pp. 13-36.
12. E.J. Mishan, *The Cost of Economic Growth*, Penguin Books, 1969, p. 225.
13. 6 November, 1957.
14. On Saturday, March 17, 1883, the *London Times* published the following notice:

    Our Paris correspondent informs us of the death of Dr. Karl Marx, which occurred last Wednesday, in London. He was born at Cologne, in the year 1818. At the age of 25 he had to leave his native country and take refuge in France, on account of the Radical opinions expressed in a paper of which he was editor. In France he gave himself up to the study of philosophy and politics, and made himself so obnoxious to the Prussian Government by his writings, that he was expelled from France, and lived for a time in Belgium. In 1847 he assisted at the Working Men's Congress in London, and was one of the authors of the "Manifesto of the Communist Party". After the Revolution of 1848 he returned to Paris, and afterwards to his native city of Cologne, from which he was again expelled for his revolutionary writings, and after escaping from imprisonment in France, he settled in London. From this time he was one of the leaders of the Socialist Party in Europe, and in 1866 he became its acknowledged chief. He wrote pamphlets on various subjects, but his chief work was *Le Capital*, an attack on the whole capitalist system. For some time he had been suffering from weak health.

What is remarkable about this piece is not only its provenance from Paris but also the way in which the class solidarity of international capital is revealed in it through reporting the concerted reactions of governments (the Prussian Government is annoyed – thus – the French Government acts) to the "obnoxiousness" of the man who dared to write "an attack on the whole capitalist system".

15. Editorial, *The Times*, 17 October, 1970.
16. Ibid., 20 October, 1970.
17. Marx's comments on the Prussian censorship instructions throw an interesting light on this "liberal" mode of arguing: "Nothing will be tolerated which opposes Christian religion in general or a particular doctrine in a frivolous and hostile manner." How cleverly put: frivolous, hostile. The adjective "frivolous" appeals to the citizen's sense of propriety and is the exoteric term in the public view; but the adjective "hostile" is whispered into the censor's ear and becomes the legal interpretation of frivolity.

In our quotation the corresponding terms are: "the influence of society" (for the citizen's sense of propriety) and "all the

power of government" (for the authoritarian state official's ear).
18. As the editors of the *Trade Union Register* rightly emphasize: The similarities between the two documents [i.e. the Tory Fair Deal at Work and Labour's In Place of Strife] are considerable, and certainly more substantial than their differences. This consensus reflects the whole tendency in orthodox political circles to assume that workers (not necessarily trade unions) have too much freedom and power in the exercise of strike action and other forms of industrial collective pressure, and that it is legitimate for the state to legislate with a view to restraining and limiting those freedoms and powers. In view of the enormous recent increases in the authority and influence of the state itself, and of large irresponsible private industrial and commercial companies, against which the independent forces of organized labour alone stand as a guarantee of ultimate civic and political liberties, the consensus view prevailing in the political parties of the centre and right requires the most vigorous and thorough opposition from the labour movement.
Trade Union Register 1970, The Merlin Press, London 1970, p. 276.
19. Barbara Castle, "The Bad Bosses Charter", *New Statesman*, 16 October 1970.
20. When Mr. Heath nationalizes Rolls Royce (after his repeated denunciation of the measure of nationalization as a "doctrinaire socialist nonsense"), all he carries out is, of course, nothing but the "nationalization" of capitalist bankruptcy in a key sector of commodity production. The fact, though, that the immediate cause of this step was a contract negotiated by the outgoing Labour Government (envisaging the balancing of enormous private losses from public funds), only highlights the surrender of both parties to the dictates of the prevailing capitalist structure of production. Such dictates prescribe the transference of the non-profitable branches of industry into the "public" (i.e.

state-bureaucracy controlled) sector so that they can be turned into further subsidies at the service of monopoly capital. Thankfully, this particular act of "nationalization" has been carried out by a Conservative Government – which makes it a less mystifying event. For had it been implemented by a Labour Government, it would have been loudly hailed as a great landmark of "pragmatic socialism".

21. Marx, *The Poverty of Philosophy*, Lawrence & Wishart, London, n.d., p. 123.
22. They are in the process of disintegration precisely because – due to their inherent contradictions – they are unable to cope with the vital functions they are supposed to carry out in the totality of social intercourse.
23. A lecture first delivered in several cities of Brazil in June 2011 and published in Portuguese in *Margem Esquerda* in 2011. First English publication in *Monthly Review*, March 2012.
24. "Breaking the US budget impasse," *The Financial Times*, June 1, 2011.
25. See my *Debate Socialista* interview (2009), republished as "The Tasks Ahead," in *The Structural Crisis of Capital*, New York: Monthly Review Press, 2010, pp. 173–202.
26. This quotation is taken from Section 18.2.1 of *Beyond Capital*, New York: Monthly Review Press, 1995, pp. 680–2
27. Sartre's interview given to the Italian Manifesto group was published as "Masses, Spontaneity, Party" in Ralph Milliband and John Saville, eds., *The Socialist Register, 1970*, London: Merlin Press, 1970, p. 245.
28. Ibid., p. 242.
29. Ibid., pp. 238–9.
30. The gravity of this problem can no longer be ignored. To realize its magnitude it is enough to quote a passage from an excellent book which offers a comprehensive account of the unfolding process of planetary destructiveness as a result of crossing some prohibitive thresholds and boundaries put into relief by environmental science:

> these thresholds have in some cases already been crossed and in other cases will soon be crossed with the

continuation of business as usual. Moreover, this can be attributed in each and every case to a primary cause: the current pattern of global socioeconomic development, that is, the capitalist mode of production and its expansionary tendencies. The whole problem can be called "the global ecological rift," referring to the overall break in the human relation to nature arising from an alienated system of capital accumulation without end. All of this suggests that the use of the term Anthropocene to describe a new geological epoch, displacing the Holocene, is both a description of a new burden falling on humanity and a recognition of an immense crisis — a potential terminal event in geological evolution that could destroy the world as we know it. On the one hand, there has been a great acceleration of the human impact on the planetary system since the Industrial Revolution, and particularly since 1945 — to the point that biogeochemical cycles, the atmosphere, the ocean, and the earth system as a whole, can no longer be seen as largely impervious to the human economy. On the other hand, the current course on which the world is headed could be described not so much as the appearance of a stable new geological epoch (the Anthropocene), as an end-Holocene, or more ominously, end-Quarternary, terminal event, which is a way of referring to the mass extinctions that often separate geological eras. Planetary boundaries and tipping points, leading to the irreversible degradation of the conditions of life on Earth, may soon be reached, science tells us, with a continuation of today's business as usual. The Anthropocene may be the shortest flicker in geological time, soon snuffed out.

John Bellamy Foster, Brett Clark, and Richard York, *The Ecological Rift: Capitalism's War on the Earth*, New York: Monthly Review Press, 2010, pp. 18–9.

31. See my Isaac Deutscher Memorial Lecture, The Necessity of Social Control, delivered at the London School of Economics on January 26, 1971. Italics in the original. Reprinted in *Beyond*

Capital, pp. 872-97. The quotation can be found on page 55 in the present volume.
32. Sartre, p. 239.
33. Rosa Luxemburg, *The Accumulation of Capital*, London: Routledge, 1963, p. 466.
34. István Mészáros, *Social Structure and Forms of Consciousness*, vol. 2: *The Dialectic of Structure and History*, New York: Monthly Review Press, 2011, p. 483.

Works by the Same Author

Satire and Reality, 1955.
La rivolta degli intellettuali in Ungheria, 1958.
Attila József e l'arte moderna, 1964.
Marx's Theory of Alienation, 1970.
The Necessity of Social Control, 1971.
Aspects of History and Class Consciousness (ed.), 1971.
Lukács's Concept of Dialectic, 1972.
Neocolonial Identity and Counter-Consciousness:
   The Work of Renato Constantino (ed.), 1978.
The Work of Sartre: Search for Freedom, 1979.
Philosophy, Ideology and Social Science, 1986.
The Power of Ideology, 1989.
Beyond Capital: Toward a Theory of Transition, 1995.
L'alternativa alla società del capitale, 2000.
Socialism or Barbarism: From the "American Century"
   to the Crossroads, 2001.
A educação para além do capital, 2005.
O desafio e o fardo do tempo histórico, 2007.
The Challenge and Burden of Historical Time, 2008.
The Structural Crisis of Capital, 2010.
Historical Actuality of the Socialist Offensive:
   Alternative to Parliamentarism, 2010.
Social Structure and Forms of Consciousness:
   vol. 1, *The Social Determination of Method*, 2010.
   vol. 2, *The Dialectic of Structure and History*, 2011.